A Mother's Love, Tested:

"Why Not Me?"

Yashica B!

Onyx Expressions Publishing

New Jersey

ISBN 978-1-7349326-2-1

Dedication

I dedicate this book to my children who have always been there for me through all the trials and tribulations. Jhevon, Donye, and Ace.

I love each of you more than you know.

To Donye, my oldest, there was certainly not a course on how to be a perfect mom, but I learned so much. In the process you taught me about life. Thank you for your love, even when it was difficult to love. You are a special young lady destined for greatness. If you ask, how do I know? I will tell you; God's grace, protection, and mercy has always been with you. You had a strong foundation and you always returned to it. Be you! Your beautiful authentic you!

MOM

Foreword

I initially met Yashica in 2020 while we were students in the Les Brown Power Voice System course. Brown is a world-renowned motivational speaker and best-selling author who is deservedly called, "The godfather of motivation and inspiration." She and I would later go on to be coached by the same coach, Jon Talarico, who is affectionally called "The Connector." Talarico has worked with many celebrities and clients all over the globe to establish himself as one of the world's foremost experts on building business relationships.

Yashica has quite a compelling story which she has outlined some parts of it in these pages that follow. As a daughter, mother, and widow, Yashica has overcome some insurmountable circumstances. Armed with these personal situations and her professional experiences as a life coach and counselor, Yashica has dedicated her life to empowering others to be the best versions of themselves.

Yashica has poured her heart and soul into healing herself and recognizes that there are many other mothers who must overcome some challenges. She offers this book as a means of letting them know that there is hope in every situation. In particular, Yashica shares some heart wrenching difficulties that she and her daughter have encountered over the years throughout their tumultuous relationship. Yashica's vulnerability and transparency to share her story is trumped only by her faith in God and her desire to empower others.

As this expedition from trauma to triumph which Yashica unfolds, be sure to remind yourself that resiliency and the ability to remain hopeful in the most difficult of situations, is possible. You are certain to be inspired by her strength, conviction, and willingness to stay the course. Her courage is unyielding and the following pages document her unwavering faith for others to ponder and consider.

This is the story of how this mother dug her heels in and fought the fight of her life. She found herself dealing with the loss of her husband as well as the realization that mental health issues were entrenched in her story. She is a true fighter in every sense of the word. Her compassion is evidenced as she releases her fears, disappointment and acknowledges this is a Spiritual fight like no other.

Being the mother of four daughters and an Ordained Minister, I was able to connect with Yashica from a mother's perspective as well as through the lenses of faith. As an Empowerment Coach, and former Counselor and Family Therapist, through Yashica's account here within,

I was reminded of the remarkable power of faith in the Lord and the devotion that comes with motherhood.

Dr. Angie Gray

Table of Contents

Introduction

———◆—◆—◆———

This book was written after my life was turned upside down once again; however, this time in a good way. This book tells the story of my love as a mother and how it was tested.

One day I was looking at my daughter as a defiant teenager whom I anticipated would soon turn into a defiant young adult. This book tells the story of how I believed that to be true and later learned that my only daughter was suffering from an undiagnosed mental health issue. I took our story, wrote it and refused to allow it to define our relationship.

This story is still being written because there are so many layers of forgiveness that have to be addressed; one layer at a time.

Life is filled with many turns, hurdles to jump, mountains to climb, and rivers to cross. One thing that forever remains the same is my faith and our family's faith in God. The fact God had us when we did not know how to have ourselves. I do feel comforted in knowing that I always operated in the "why not me" mindset. I always believed as long as it was me to experience the complicated turns, hurdles, mountains, and rivers that came with living then it would mean perhaps that someone else would not have to endure the harsh experiences that come with living in order to learn the lessons I learned. I can now share those lessons and prayerfully, help someone who needs to know they are not alone. I have always been ok. Looking back, I know "He favored me;" how else could I have made it?

As you read this story of my experience, reflect on your own life. I can almost guarantee you, God carried you in the midst of it all as my cousin Emerald Stone writes.

Part 1

———◆◆◆———

I understand that forgiveness is not about forgetting. Forgiveness is remembering without anger and rage.

Many believe children are gifts. I believe children are a gift only to those who pray, prepare, plan and want them. At an early age, I knew I was different in the way I thought about having children. I really did not want to have any children and especially not naturally from my body. After getting older, I decided I wanted to adopt two children. As a young girl and teenager, growing up in the Baptist church, I was never the one to go look at any babies in church. I did not *ooh* and *ahh* over any baby, toddler, or child. It just was not in me. I would stand off to the side or stay in the back. My friends and cousins looked on and played with new babies with such love and excitement. Not me. I seriously looked from a distance and was not remotely interested.

It was not until I had my first child, a baby girl, that changed my thinking. Funny thing is, I had always thought I would adopt and God said, "Nope, you will carry and birth your own children out of your body." I delivered my daughter as anticipated, but with a set of issues. Labor was difficult. I carried the baby perfectly, but when it was time to deliver, my body would not turn her loose. My birthing canal barely opened, and my cervix would not dilate more than a centimeter. If you have had children, most likely you are understanding the agony and pain I was in. My contractions were on top of each other; fast and extremely hard. I thought I was about to give birth at any moment. But, much to my surprise this birth would be prolonged.

After several failed attempts to make my cervix dilate, a decision had to be made. You see, once a baby is in the birthing canal it is ready to leave its mother's body. My daughter was ready to meet the world and unfortunately, her mother's body was holding her hostage. "What do most people do when they are feeling locked up with no way out?" They panic and some even retreat. That is exactly what my daughter did. She was moving into what the doctors called fetal distress. Fetal distress is an emergency in which a baby experiences oxygen deprivation. I was a young mom, only 20 years old. My mom, sister, and husband were looking on in disbelief and not really knowing what was going on. I remember the doctor explaining to my husband and mom that because of the distress, time was of the essence. The baby had to come out or she could possibly die because she was now in distress. She was trying to turn around and go back into my uterus. At this point, I now have a team of doctors in the room trying to decide what the next course of action should be. The suggestion from the team of doctors, was for me to have an emergency C-section, right then and there! Time was not on my side. With each passing moment, the risk of losing her was greater. I vaguely remember their faces. I heard the doctor say, "We need to put the mother to sleep." Can you imagine that? I found myself thinking, "This is my first child, and I have to have a C-section and be put to sleep." I was in so much pain that I was fading in and out. Honestly, I don't truly remember who made the decision. Trust me, at the point of pain that I was experiencing, I did not care! I do remember asking them to please do something – anything to alleviate the pain. At that moment, I learned I have a very low tolerance for pain. I was hurting so bad I could not stay focused or conscious. Also, to add to the misery of knowing I had to have a C-section, I was not given anything for pain.

So much was happening so fast, and yet, it seemed I was moving in slow motion. I seemed to be having an out-of-body experience. I remember seeing myself on the transfer bed, but I saw myself as a spectator, not the actual person lying there with an oxygen mask on my face. I do not know how long I was there because I did not have a concept of time. When I woke up, I did not even know if my baby was alive. I had not received her in the birthing room. I was confused because I had not yet heard her cry. I had not yet seen her. In fact, I did not even see my husband, mom, or sister. I felt like something was awry. I was twenty-years-old, had seen my sister's delivery, and watched enough deliveries on TV shows to know something was not right. From what I knew, I thought a nurse was supposed to put the baby next to me. I had envisioned smiling and taking pictures with my new baby.

None of that happened. I was in the room all by myself. I was alone and confused as to where everyone was.

Are you thinking, *"Where was everyone and why was I alone?"* Since I was still on active duty in the Army stationed in Germany and had returned home to have my child, I was assigned to Keesler Air Force Base. I had my baby in an actual operating room, not a labor & delivery room, therefore, standard operating procedures were enforced; only medical staff members and the patient were permitted in the operating room.

Minutes seemed like hours before the nurse came and told me I was going to be moved to my room. I asked, "What did I have, a boy or a girl?" She smiled and said, "A healthy baby girl with a head full of hair." I was relieved. I had previously opted not to know the sex of the baby before birth. I remember thinking to myself, *"Wow, I have a healthy little girl."*

Once I was moved to the recovery room, I learned that my mother and sister were in the waiting room. Obviously, the time had passed. I just did not realize how much because I had been sedated with anesthesia. My husband was in the infant room with our daughter. He was able to put her on his chest, FIRST. She heard his heartbeat outside my body FIRST, not MINE!

As I reflect on that September day in 1995, I am compelled to share the many changes that have occurred. Fast-forward; my daughter is now twenty-five years old. My husband and I divorced when she was only 3 years old. I remained affiliated with the military and had multiple missions that took me away from her. Eventually, I married again and added two boys to our family. In 2010 my second husband was diagnosed with *Amyotrophic Lateral Sclerosis* (ALS), also known as Lou Gehrig's Disease. The disease affects the muscles of the body. It is like having a stroke except your stroke is in your spinal cord in which the central nervous system controls all movement. In ALS patients' muscles begin to deteriorate and ultimately die, causing paralysis until eventually, all muscles including the diaphragm die and no longer function. That and other complications eventually lead to death.

This time in our family's life was very difficult as we were all trying to adjust and prepare for the inevitable. The disease progression was so rapid that we barely kept up. His physical deterioration was difficult to anticipate and effectively deal with. I was trying to manage the household with an infant, a nine-year-old, a 15-year-old, and a terminally ill husband. As you might imagine, it was definitely not a *walk in the park*. It was quite challenging on a lot of fronts. It was tough for all of us. I am certain that the responsibility put on the kids to help must have been stressful and scary for them as well. Ultimately, he passed away in 2012 as a result of this disease. Not only did I lose a husband, but my children also lost their father. My daughter who was 16 years old when he passed was devastated because she was losing another father. She had claimed her step-father and loved him as her own.

After my husband passed away the relationship between my daughter and me turned sour. We loved each other as mother and daughter, but we did not seem to like one another. About two months after my husband's passing, we had an argument and my daughter just walked out of the house and left home. She walked out while I was still talking to her. Now, I am a *black momma,* and any momma can probably relate to how my blood was boiling at that moment. That is something we usually do not tolerate! However, I did. You see, I was a cross between a traditional *black momma* raised in the south and a modern young momma who tried to be understanding. I could relate because I was somewhat detached myself. However, this girl was gone for a couple of days without a phone call, text, or letter; no contact. Then, she suddenly returned. She didn't say anything when she returned and neither did I. Believe it or not, I said nothing. I do not know what thoughts I was having. This situation was so complicated that I found myself speechless, so I said nothing. She came back and carried on as if nothing ever happened. She acted like she was not just gone for three days, and I allowed her to do so. I still don't know why I let her get away with that.

This defiant behavior continued, but the disappearing acts did not show up again until two years later. She was a college student living in South Carolina. I had eventually moved back to South Carolina as well. I wanted to be close to her and back at the place my husband and I loved so much. While we were in separate states our relationship was that of a typical mother and daughter. She missed me and I missed her. Once her brothers and I moved to South Carolina, the relationship went sour again. Over the course of about two years she would stay with me. Something would happen and she would get mad and just disappear again. As this behavior continued, she would call after a few days and ask me to come get her or to send her money so she could get home. This was happening a lot until one day I just told her, "No more." I suggested she stay on the other side of the door because the behavior was not welcomed, and it was such a bad influence on my younger sons. It was heartbreaking to see my little one's face after he looked for his sister and waited for her to return. I was convinced she was on drugs. *What else could explain this behavior?*

It became evident that this situation was escalating and affecting my entire family. I realized that something had to be done. There were so many possible reasons for the behavior. I had so many questions going through my mind. Was she just reacting to her father's death? Was she using drugs? Was it because we never truly bonded? Was it because she needed boundaries? Was it because she did not like me and I did not like her? Was it because she could tell that I was detached? I ruminated on the fact that I had never wanted to have children. I kept asking myself what could I do differently.

I set boundaries and told her that she could not keep leaving home and coming back whenever she felt like it. Although I would say for her not to come back, I still allowed her to come and leave again several times; disregarding the boundary I had supposedly set. I had a hard time enforcing the boundary. I began making excuses and believing them. She bonded with her father, but not with me. I had convinced myself that a lot of the problem was that we just didn't like each other. Sure, we loved each other; we just did not like each other. Those were my thoughts and that is what I believed. I convinced myself that she was not connected to me and I was not connected to her. This was easy to believe at this point. It was not just easy to believe, I wanted to believe it. There simply was no evidence that a bond existed between us. Of course, I realized that not every mother-daughter relationship is like the one that Claire Huxtable, Denise, & Saundra from the Cosby Show had. Once I settled on that, I thought it would be okay. I accepted that as my truth. This idea worked for me for a while. And then...

On March 1, 2020, tensions were high in my household. My daughter, with her *shenanigans* as I call them, left again. This time was different though, it had darkness over it. Unlike previous times, I cared, and I was actually scared for her. I placed that dreadful call to 9-1-1 and reported a missing person. The detectives came to my house, took my statement, and gathered information; her name, height, weight, hair color, a picture, etc. They assured me they would do the best they could to find her.

The police officers were not gone from my home more than ten minutes before I received a phone call that would again change my life forever. My son was in a solo car accident in Fairfield County and was being medevacked to Richland County Trauma Hospital. That was the first time in my life I broke down. For a moment, it felt like my heart stopped beating and my chest could not rise. I lost control! I thought I had lost two children in

17

the same night within minutes of each other. I couldn't believe this was happening.

My eleven-year-old son held me as I cried uncontrollably. He knew something serious was happening because he had never seen *his rock, his protector, his mom,* like that. I called out to heaven and thankfully angels showed up. All my life I knew I was strong and had endured a great deal of pain up until this point without breaking down. Was everything I had been through prepping me for this moment, I asked God? One thing I did not ask Him was, *"Why me?"* Instead, I asked him, *"Why not* me?" I knew if it was me then someone else would be spared. I always seemed to be more concerned with others than with myself. With all the challenges in my life I asked God the same thing, but this time I asked for more strength. I needed it for my eleven-year-old. I had to leave him at home and confused while I went to the trauma center. As I write this, the memories make me realize that everyone – even me has a breaking point. Although the details escape me, the memories still show me that sometimes we must lean on the angels to carry us through. And I am okay with that. I have enough faith to know the angels will not leave me out there on my own.

I was traveling to the hospital with angels carrying me all the way. Thankfully, other angels were dispatched and beat us to the hospital. This is important because I did not call and activate these angels. God assigned the mission to someone else. He took care of everything. Remember, I was crying and moaning as my 11-year-old held me when I received the phone call. I am moving quickly through the story and as you read you are probably asking yourself; *Where is my youngest son? Was my daughter found? Did my oldest son survive the accident?* Great questions. My youngest son was taken by yet another angel to be comforted at her home and yes, my oldest son lived through the accident. He sustained many broken bones, and thankfully, has recovered completely.

Meanwhile, in the midst of the crisis with my son, heaven shined upon us and there was light. My daughter was found safe and sound that night. Shortly thereafter my daughter was hospitalized. During her hospitalization on the mental health floor, I received good news. My daughter was diagnosed with a mental illness. Yes, I said *good* news because at least now I have an explanation and reason for all the hatefulness and unacceptable behavior I endured over the years. I finally realized that she had been struggling with a mental illness. All these years we had no idea what was going on in her head. It was comforting to realize that these behaviors were a result of mental illness. It was not her fault or mine. Unbeknownst to us, it was a part of her condition which had not been diagnosed.

Her behavior resulted from her not understanding the thoughts she was experiencing. I had chalked it up to a defiant teenager that hated her mother and later became a young adult that hated her mother. Fortunately, none of that was actually true. Had we caught the disorder early, this chapter would have read differently.

Think about this quote by Les Brown, *"When life knocks you down, try to land on your back. Because if you can look up, you can get up."* From my life's journey, I would add "Once you get up, do something different." That is what I had to do… "something different." I had to retrain my thoughts and forgive the behaviors of the defiant teenager, turned young adult, and see her again as my loving daughter. Like the words of Donnie

McClurkin's hit gospel song says, *"We fall down, but we get up. For a saint is just a sinner who fell down and got back up,"* my daughter fell down and got back up.

Now she knows something different; and so do I. We look and live in this life and oftentimes what we see is not what we initially believe it to be. In general, society (myself included) tends to attribute the type of behavior that she was exhibiting to that of drug abuse. While mental illness shares some of the same symptoms that resemble the behaviors of a drug abuser; it often goes overlooked, and the resulting behaviors are believed to be accepted as drug abuse instead. My guess is that this is because we do not know how mental illness presents itself. Now that I know better, I challenge you, the reader, to take it upon yourself to learn and be knowledgeable of what behaviors a person experiencing mental illness may exhibit. I think about my daughter and how it must have been for her, being trapped inside for all those years with nowhere to retreat. She could not bring herself out and I could not help her. I could not help her because I didn't know any better either. I wish I had considered the fact that it could be something other than drug abuse. If I had even thought about mental illness, it would have at least given me another angle to analyze the behaviors.

The process of undoing the damage that was done will prove to be long and daunting, but I am certain it will be worth it. Not only did I have to learn to adjust and forgive, but so did other family members. My daughter's behavior impacted all of us. She is in the process of learning to forgive herself and embracing her perceived self-worth. My daughter deserves a peaceful life and I believe that is why God gave her a *"Why not me?" mom* to help her. Together, we are learning to understand that life happens and we do not have to look at life as what is happening *to* us. If we merely change our thoughts, we can look at life as it happens *for* us. The lesson we have learned is that it is better to identify the root of the problem and then work together to find a viable solution. This mindset shift can change our lives and how we interpret and live our life.

Part 2

P.A.I.D. In Full

———————◆—◆—◆———————

According to Dr. Dharius Daniels, the greatest pains and the greatest joys come from the same place - *relationships*. I can attest to that statement because I have experienced, what seems like, an infinite amount of both. While I have often been confused along the way on my journey, I know for a fact that relationships are challenging, but these challenges can be minimized. Having discussed the volatile relationship I had with my daughter at the beginning of this writing, I feel obligated to share the solution that I found. Armed with the new information of my daughter's diagnosis, I began to take a look at our situation from a different perspective. I began to examine my own belief system.

Even though she does have a mental illness, I realized it is only fair if I do some soul searching. In doing so, I devised a practice that allowed me to find some peace of mind. Since that time, I have used this practice in many different situations in my life. I call it *P.A.I.D. in Full.* (**P**ray. **A**cknowledge and accept an **I**ntentional **D**eliverance). In following the ideas of this formula, I have been able to find some peace of mind. I am sharing it here because I believe it could possibly help you as well when you encounter challenging situations and circumstances.

"P" is to *pray*. Without prayer, there would not be forgiveness. One thing I know for sure is that prayer definitely changes things. I believe that it is because of prayer that I had a change of heart. It helped me to see the importance of introspection which led me to the realization that forgiveness was necessary for healing.

Without forgiveness for my daughter, my mother, and myself, the healing process could not begin. So, it is because of prayer that I was able to forgive and can now heal. I knew I needed to pray, but I just could not. It was like I was reaching for a lifeline, but could not bring myself to it. Although many people believe that prayer is easy, I'm here to acknowledge that praying is not necessarily easy. In fact, I was so hurt and disappointed, that I felt like it was impossible to pray. My best friend and others interceded for me until I was able to pray for myself. Without those prayers from her and others, I do not know where we would be. Those intercessory prayers sustained me until I was able to pray for myself. I was of the belief that you had to pray a certain way. I thought you had to pray while down on your knees with your eyes closed. Then, I learned that how you pray only matters to you and God. The most important thing is that you actually pray, not how you pray. Praying hours on your knees like the deacons in the old Baptist church did not bring any more results than it did when I got comfortable with God...When I talked to Him on my terms, in my own way. I developed an intimate relationship with God and learned to simply talk with Him through prayer and listen for His voice through meditation. These practices began my healing process and led me to the answers I needed.

After praying for answers I had to "A" (*acknowledge and accept*); that my daughter has a mental illness, and that our relationship was what it was, but we must now move forward. We must do the heart work in order to improve ourselves individually as well as our relationship. We both believe that with a conscientious effort, we can improve our relationship. This acknowledgment changed things for me. Acknowledging and accepting that I must put in the hard work and the heart work, gave me some clarity about the undoing of the past in order to create a healthier future. I acknowledge and accept that this is an on-going process. Healing is not going to happen without doing the work and certainly will not happen overnight. My prayers for answers revealed that having self-reflection and willingness to do the work, will benefit both of us.

Beyond learning to acknowledge and accept things the way they were, I also learned that it is important to be intentional in my prayer life. This brings us to the "I." While I had prayed for many hours, I had not been intentional. It became clear to me that my prayer life could be stronger and more effective if I actually prayed with intention. While I managed to keep an open connection with God, it was distant. I believe it was distant because I was not being clear about what I really wanted. When I understood that, I learned to pray for exactly what I wanted. I also learned that when you pray intentional prayers you must have faith that they will be answered. I know that the Word tells us that prayers are answered, but sometimes they don't seem to be answered the way you think they will be or in the timeframe you think they should be. In looking at what I discovered previously about perspective, I came to understand that intentional prayers are answered, but not necessarily in the way that you have asked them to be answered. God answers prayer in a way that is in our best interest, even if we don't realize it yet. He will not answer your prayer if it is not going to ultimately be good for you. I now know that I should have been praying for deliverance from my own issues. Once I prayed with intention, the Lord led me to look at myself and my own issues that stem from my relationship with my mother.

In implementing this formula, I came to terms with another reality. I realized that I was missing something in my own childhood. It became clear to me that, over the years, I had been seeking validation from my own mother. It was evidenced in the choices I made, the life I lived, and the way I viewed having children. Unfortunately, I never felt validated. I believe this may be why I found myself feeling detached.

As I began to contemplate and examine the root of this detachment, I recognized that I had to first forgive myself and then forgive my mother. I decided that not only must I forgive my daughter for her behavior I also had to forgive my mother because I felt unloved. I also had to forgive myself for not recognizing that my daughter was experiencing a mental illness. Forgiveness is not easy, but it is necessary. In forgiving, I realize that being non-judgmental is crucial. It is easy to pass judgment on others but this is the wrong approach, especially when you do not have all the facts. I now recognize that parenting is not easy. In fact, it can be downright difficult. Acknowledging this actually made it easier for me to forgive my mother.

The intentional prayers were for the next letter "D" for *deliverance*. I now realized I had to be delivered from myself. What I mean by that is that although my daughter had her issues, many of them were actually related to my own issues. After we began the healing process and the smoke cleared I was able to see myself in my daughter. It seemed like it was me staring in the mirror looking back at me. I could relate to how she must have been feeling. Self-awareness is a key ingredient to reviving any relationship. The only person that can heal you is yourself and it begins by traveling down those dark paths in your life. It means facing the reality that you have unresolved issues from the past that may be getting in the way of your current relationships. We all have them. In order to deal with your issues, you must first acknowledge and accept them.

Then you must decide to deal with them and determine how you will do so. You must be intentional in your approach. I chose a spiritual faith-based approach to heal by **P**raying, **A**cknowledging, being **I**ntentional, and seeking **D**eliverance (*P.A.I.D. in Full*). By doing this, my hope was that my daughter would watch me closely and that she would see the path and follow it as well. In doing so, she would have to forgive herself and heal in her own unique way. I realize that I can only heal myself; I cannot heal her. The best I can do is show her that I'm willing to do the necessary work and encourage her to be willing to follow suit.

Together, we are using the *P.A.I.D. in Full* method to heal ourselves and our relationship. I must acknowledge that sometimes the past seeps into our present and I find myself bringing up old issues and baggage. I'm happy to acknowledge that I got the chance to see her demonstrate her growth. One day I was riding in the car with my daughter and an unwanted spirit came over me. I was still a little bitter and things were still hurting and bothering me inside. Now and then it showed its ugly face. The spirit wanted to bring up the past and I wanted to remind my daughter of something she did. My daughter politely said, "Mom, can we please just move forward and not go backward?" I know this may happen occasionally and should be expected in the healing process, but it helped that she reminded me to let it go. This time was different; she spoke to me in a respectful way. It meant a lot to me because I could see that she really was trying to work on our relationship. That was her maturity coming into play and my divine directive to reset my thinking to a positive state. It made me realize that you cannot see what is in front of you while you are looking in the rear-view mirror. It was good to know that she had been paying attention and listening to all the self-help lessons and books I had been sharing with her.

As I reflect on where we have come from in our relationship, I realize that sometimes we simply are not clear about what is happening in our lives. We think one thing, but it is something completely different. I remember the etching in the side view mirror of my mom's Buick, that read, *Objects in mirrors are closer than they appear.* With that in mind, my daughter and I have decided to design a life that we can both enjoy. We are committed to living a *P.A.I.D. in Full* life together. We know it is work but certainly, work worth doing. Every day is a step closer and each day is worth it. As I reflect on this, I remind myself that I am a *"Why not me?"* mom.

"Have Your Roses Now"
Special Acknowledgements

As I reflect back on March 1, 2020, I realize that it is a date I will never forget. I cannot forget that date because it is the night I briefly lost both of my children, Nacoria Donye and Jhevon Tyre. In the previous pages of this book, I referenced angels that had intervened on my behalf. There were several people that showed up for me and offered assistance with no expectations or conditions. I would like to thank them and acknowledge them. My world was shaken, rocked, split, and placed back together. Without them I do not know how I would have made it.

My sister, Lawanna, I still cannot remember if I called her or if she just happened to have called me, but she was there for me when I needed her. While she was 8 hours and hundreds of miles away, she did her best to come to my aid. Despite the distance, she managed to navigate the situation and get the necessary help and pieces pulled together.

My sister, Shelonyna, talked to me in the late-night hours thru the early morning. I could hear in her voice that she was empathetic and that she recognized how I was hurting internally. I was in pain and quite a distance away from any of my family. I knew she could relate because she had been through a similar situation, but I was torn, devastated, and exhausted. While I was comforted by her voice; I still felt like I was alone and that my world was crashing down around me.

My neighbors Judelka and Regina, both provided love and comfort for my youngest son, Ace. Although it was late, neither of them questioned or complained about taking care of him.

My neighbors Gina and Tamarjio, soon jumped in and, without hesitation, became my chauffeur. Because they were concerned about my mental state following this hard blow, they wanted to do everything they could to help and ensure my safety.

Jackie and Robert Pitt, I tear up writing this. I am so appreciative for how you so willingly stopped whatever you were doing to provide my transportation to the hospital. You all refused to let me go alone. You brought comfort and a certain peace with you that I didn't even have to ask for.

Dominic Robinson-Neal, Sr. our relationship is just different and at times I do not think even we understand it. I have to recognize you and say that I am forever grateful for you because in spite of the fact that we argue, disagree and oftentimes do not even speak to one another, that night when you received the call that Jhevon needed you, you became a superhero and was there before anyone else. You were his constant male role model, friend, and father figure throughout the entire ordeal. We all thank you and Andrea for being there, for checking on us, for providing transportation for us. I especially thank you because I did not have to worry about if he had someone there because you always showed up without any expectations. You were there. Thank you!

Paige, you need a book of "thank you" all by yourself. There are many words in the English language to express gratitude and appreciation. You deserve them all. You were there for our family – each one of us. You were our inside "rock." I had two children experience trauma at the same time, and I could not physically be in both places at the same time. You, Paige, demonstrated such dedication and commitment to our family. You were determined to fill in the gap by staying by Jevon's side day and every night he was in the hospital and then recovering at home. To be so young you set the example of what unconditional love looks like and what through sickness and in health really means. Thank you!

All of you played such roles in our lives that night and in the weeks and months to follow that I had to "give you your roses now." You deserve so much more than I could ever give; but please know that I thank you so much! Thank you for being who you are now and who you were that night. I unequivocally acknowledge each of you as God's Angels.

Yashica B!

About The Author

<u>Yashica B. Mack</u>

Yashica Broughton Mack is a Self-Development professional who specializes in working with individuals, as well as entrepreneurs, in developing stronger, more productive relationships.

Yashica believes that understanding your inner-self, and acknowledging the self-talk working inside of you, makes the difference in becoming the better "YOU".

Yashica is an Army Veteran from Theodore, Alabama, who discovered how to live a *P.A.I.D. in Full* life by coming to terms with, and understanding *"life happens."* Yashica lost her husband, a 23-year Army Veteran, in 2012 from a neurodegenerative terminal illness, Amyotrophic Lateral Sclerosis (ALS), better known to many as *Lou Gehrig's Disease.*

Yashica is a graduate of Troy University, obtaining a Bachelor's degree in Psychology, as well as a Master's degree in Counseling and Psychology, a Certified Life Coach, a Certified Les Brown Power Voice Speaker, and an active member of the American Association of Christian Counselors.

Yashica has worked with many professionals in an array of career and personal fields, from professional athletes, other counselors, and military personnel. She has been featured in IMARA Woman Magazine, sports media outlets such as ADSN and World Combat Sports, Kiss

FM, local news outlets like WLTX 19, and the 2020 Power Summit with the world's greatest influential motivation speaker, Mr. Les Brown and his team.

Yashica combined her education, training, and experience in becoming the *Eclectic Mindset Motivator*, enriching relationships, and managing the eclectic mind across the Americas, and soon the globe.

Yashica is a dedicated mother of three children, committed to living the best version of herself and teaching her children, as well as the world, to do the same.

Her motto is, "You do not have to tear down anyone's kingdom while building your empire. There is plenty of room at the top; it is the bottom that is crowded!"

Yashica B!

Contact Information

https://www.facebook.com/yashicaB4U

https://www.instagram.com/yashicab4u/

https://www.linkedin.com/in/yashica-mack-a400928b/

https://twitter.com/Yashica95

www.YashicaB.com

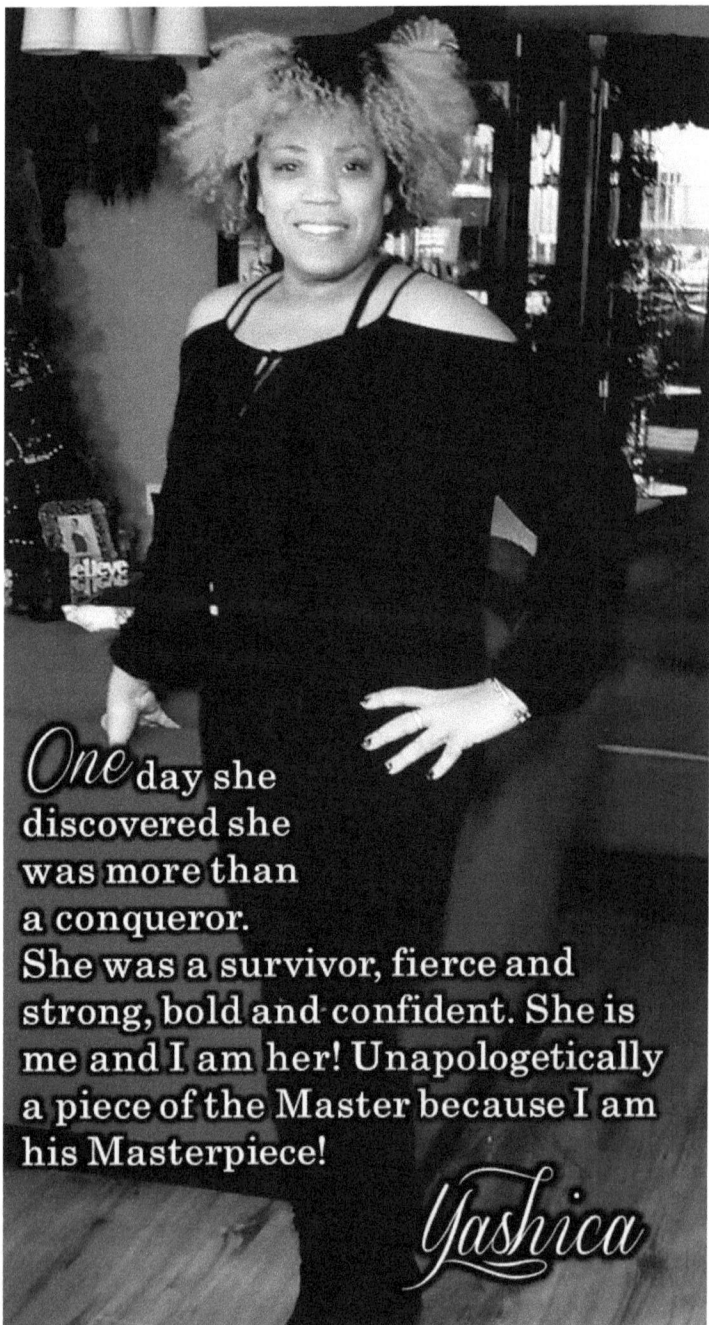

One day she discovered she was more than a conqueror. She was a survivor, fierce and strong, bold and confident. She is me and I am her! Unapologetically a piece of the Master because I am his Masterpiece!

Yashica